# BUILD A BOOK

Get ready to BUILD A BOOK! Build a Book for Boys is full of fun exercises that will introduce you to creative writing. Get ready to use your imagination and discover the writer within!

## Helpful hints for getting started:

On these pages you'll find lots of ideas to help you get started, plus plenty of space for writing. Start at the beginning of the book and try to work through the activities in order. If you get stuck, there are story prompts to inspire you. Try not to worry too much about spelling and handwriting at this stage; you can perfect those later on. And don't forget to use your stickers as you finish the activities!

pencil    sharpener    eraser    this book!

# The Author!

Write about yourself on this page.

Draw a picture of yourself in the frame.

Name: _____

_____

Age: _____

_____

What do you look like?
Describe your
physical characteristics.
For example, what
color is your hair? What
color are your eyes?

_____

_____

_____

_____

_____

Now write down some adjectives that describe
your personality.

_____

_____

_____

# My Future

On this page, write about your hopes and dreams for the future.
What do you wish for? What do you want to be when you are older?

Way
to go!

# My Best Buddy

Draw a picture of your best friend.

## My Best Buddy

Describe what kind of person he/she is and what you like the most about him/her.

_____

_____

_____

_____

_____

_____

_____

# My Favorite Books

On this page, write a list of your favorite books.
Don't forget to include the authors!

You
did it!

# Cover to Cover

Choose your favorite book and redesign the cover.

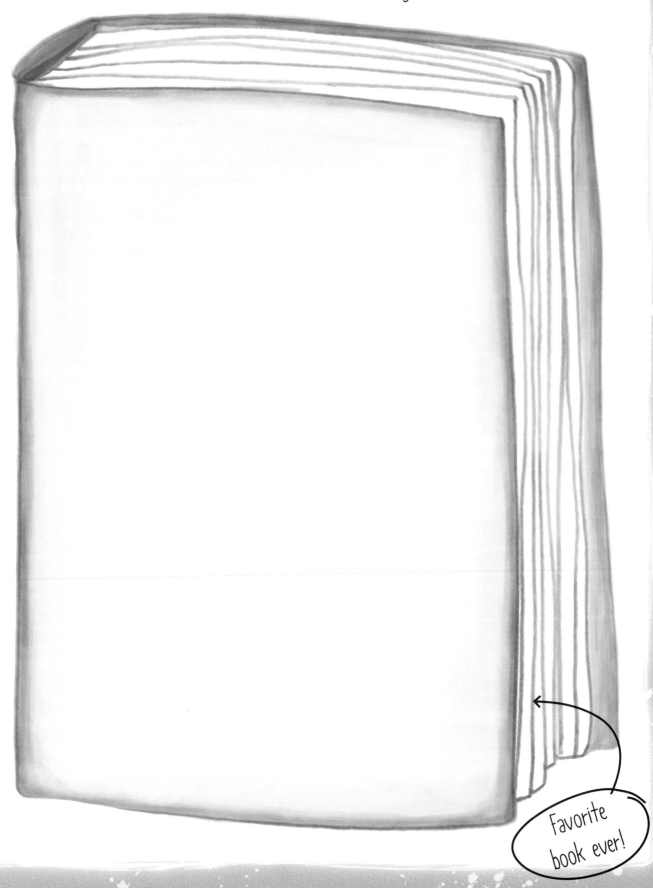

Favorite book ever!

# I Love it Because . . .

Write about what you love about your favorite book.

This is my favorite book because _____
_____
_____
_____
_____

My favorite character is _____
I like him/her because _____
_____
_____

My favorite part of the book is _____
_____
_____
_____
_____

My least favorite part of the book is _____
_____
_____
_____
_____
_____
_____

Fantastic!

# "Wow" Words

The best kind of writing has lots of different, interesting words. For example, was it **big** or was it **colossal**? Are you **hungry** or are you **ravenous**? We call these words **"wow"** words. They are most commonly known as adjectives.

Why not borrow a thesaurus and create a list of your own "wow" words?

Did your character <u>say</u> something, or was it: GROANED

BOASTED  MUMBLED  GASPED  YAWNED

YELLED

SHRIEKED  CRIED  WHISPERED

SCREAMED  SIGHED  SHOUTED

Is your character <u>bad</u>, or is he/she:

VILE  ATROCIOUS

FOUL  VILLAINOUS

DESTRUCTIVE  SPITEFUL

WICKED  VICIOUS  CORRUPT

Was it <u>good</u> or was it:

ASTONISHING

MIND-BLOWING  EXHILARATING  WONDROUS

BREATHTAKING  THRILLING  OVERWHELMING

# Amazing Adjectives

On this page write at least two adjectives for each letter.
...uple have been done for you. If you get stuck, you can refer to a dictionary.

**a**

**b**

**c**
clumsy

**d**

**e**

**f**

**g**
generous

**h**

**i**
imaginative

**j**

**k**
knightly

**l**

**m**

**n**

**o**

**p**

**q**
quiet

**r**

**s**

**t**
talkative

**u**

**v**
vacant

**w**

**y**
yummy

**z**

**x** is missing because there aren't many adjectives beginning with this letter!

Amazing!

# Fantastic Soccer Player

Label the soccer player with "wow" words.
If you are struggling, look at some of the adjectives
at the bottom of the page for inspiration.

SLOW

FAST

NIMBLE

SKILLFUL

LAZY

SPORTY

Using some of the words that you chose, write a little bit about the soccer player. Imagine he's a character taking part in a soccer competition.

_____

_____

_____

_____

_____

Here are some useful questions to ask yourself when developing a character:

- What is his/her name?
- How old is he/she?
- What does he/she look like?
- What does he/she do?
- What kind of person is he/she?
- What are his/her likes/dislikes?
- How old is he/she?
- What is his/her secret wish?
- Who are his/her friends?

Once you can answer some of these questions, you'll have a better idea of the kind of character he/she is!

Way to go!

# Splendid Superhero

Create your own superhero in the space below. Around the outside write lots of adjectives to describe him/her. For example, is he/she courageous or a scaredy cat? What is his/her superhero power?

My **SUPERHERO's** name is _____

Use the adjectives you came up with to
write about your superhero. Imagine he is
part of a story and try to answer these questions:

- Who is he going to save?
- How is he going to save the day?
- Who tries to stop him?
- Does he succeed?

Don't forget to use plenty of
"wow" words. Here are a few
to get you started:
spectacular **super**
AWESOME
**exhilarating** magnificent

You
did it!

# The Missing Sidekick

Colin the cowboy has lost his trusty steed. On the lines, write as many words as you can think of that describe how you think he might be feeling.

Fantastic!

# Missing!

Don't forget, not all characters are human! Complete this poster for Colin's missing sidekick. Don't forget to add as many details as you can — they don't just have to be physical characteristics, you can also include information about what he/she likes or dislikes.

Name: _____

Age: _____

Description: _____

_____

_____

_____

Where he/she was last seen: _____

# My Pet Dragon

You have been given a dragon as a pet. Accessorize him/her and write some "wow" words around the outside to describe his/her personality. Don't forget to give your pet a name!

Now write about the physical characteristics:

What color is he/she? _____

_____

How does he/she feel to touch? _____

_____

How does he/she smell? _____

_____

# Dragon Adventures

On this page, write about an adventure you could have with your pet dragon.

_____

_____

_____

_____

_____

_____

_____

_____

_____

## Story Prompts:

- Is he/she a friendly dragon?
- Does he/she have a magical power? For example, can he/she fly?
- Is anybody chasing after him/her?
- Is he/she protecting something?

Amazing!

# The When and Where

Now that you've looked at characters, it's time to look at story settings. This is when and where they take place. Below are some examples — try adding a couple more to each list.

## WHEN

Fall

Spring

The morning

The afternoon

100 years in the future

## WHERE

In the Wild West

In a haunted castle

In a closet under the stairs

In the jungle

# The Four Seasons

Think of at least four adjectives to describe each of the seasons below.
Try not to think too hard about it—write whatever comes into your head.
Remember, it's not just about the weather!

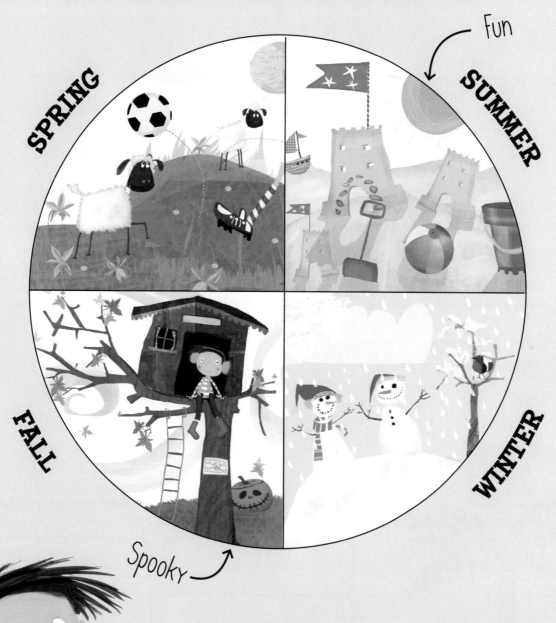

Fun

SPRING

SUMMER

FALL

WINTER

Spooky

Do any of these seasons
inspire you to write a story?
At the back of the book,
write down your ideas!

Way
to go!

# Wish You Were Here!

On the postcard, draw a picture of either your favorite place to be, or somewhere that you would like to go.

Write five adjectives that describe your scene:

Write the postcard to your best friend.
Don't forget to include the following details:

- Where you are
- What you have done

- What it is like
- What you are going to do

When describing your surroundings, always remember your five senses: what you can **see**, **hear**, **touch**, **taste**, and **smell**. Mention all of these things and you will transport the reader into your imagination!

You did it!

# The Science Lab

Where does this scientist work? Draw his lab below!

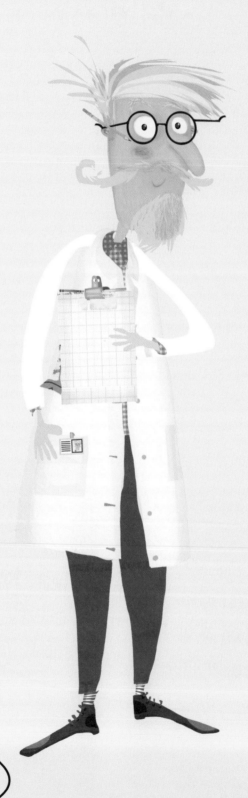

When writing a story, sometimes it helps to draw your setting!

Fantastic!

# Potion Problems

Describe the scientist's laboratory. Don't forget your five senses!

# Lost!

Aliens that have landed in your hometown have lost their spaceship.
In the "missing" poster, draw a picture of the spaceship and describe it underneath.

# Aliens Have Landed

Describe your encounter with the aliens.

Amazing!

# Planning Your Story

You've thought about your characters and know when and where a story could take place. Now it's time to start planning your story. The best way to do this is with a story arc.

## THE BUILD-UP

Introduce a potential problem and start to build the tension. This is where the story takes off!

_Start here_

## CHARACTERS

Before you start thinking about what happens in your story, think about who's going to be in it. Who is the main character?

## THE BEGINNING

This is where you need to introduce the characters and describe the setting.

Way to go!

Read the text below and fill in the boxes. If you're struggling, here are some story prompts you could try:

- You and your best friend discover a secret portal.
- A secret agent approaches you and asks for help in solving a crime.
- A long lost relative has left you one million dollars.

## THE PROBLEM

The problem from the previous step is now fully developed. This is where you want the drama!

_____
_____
_____
_____
_____
_____
_____
_____
_____

## THE RESOLUTION

This is where your problem needs to be resolved and for the characters to be made happy again.

_____
_____
_____
_____
_____
_____
_____
_____
_____
_____
_____

## THE ENDING

Tie up all the loose ends to finish your story.

_____
_____
_____
_____
_____
_____
_____
_____
_____

# The Secret Map

Milo and Joey have stumbled upon an undiscovered island.
Draw a map of the island. Don't forget to label it! The more detail you add,
the easier it will be when writing your story.

Is there any buried treasure?

What is the name of this island?

Don't forget the sea!

# All Aboard!

Now write about their experience.

_____

_____

_____

_____

_____

_____

_____

_____

_____

_____

_____

_____

_____

_____

_____

## Story Prompts:

- Are they searching for someone/something?
- Do they meet any mysterious characters?
- Is something hidden on the island?

You did it!

# I Spy

Write a list of items you think this spy needs to catch criminals.

# The Detective

Use your story arc to answer these questions:

- Who is the spy?
- What happens?
- What is he looking for?
- What happens at the end?

## Story Prompts:

- Does the detective get fooled by any thieves?
- Does the criminal have something of value?
- Is the spy good at his job?
- Is the criminal clumsy?

Fantastic!

# A Knight's Tale

A princess is in need of a brave knight to save her. Select three of the six words below to describe the knight. Then draw a picture of him.

COURAGEOUS

HEROIC

FEARLESS

LAZY

BRAVE

WEAK

Write some more adjectives that describe him.

# The Rescue

Using a story arc, write about your knight's attempts to save the princess.

_____

_____

_____

_____

_____

_____

_____

_____

_____

_____

_____

_____

_____

_____

_____

_____

_____

**Story Prompts:**

- How did the princess get there?
- Why is she being held hostage?
- How is the knight going to save her?

Amazing!

# Time Travel

You've been transported to the future!
Write a journal of your experience.

Date:

Way
to go!

# Comic Strip Capers

A comic strip is a series of drawings arranged in panels.

1

2

3

4

What's going on in the comic strips? Write a couple sentences to match each picture. If you like, you can add speech bubbles too!

Nice job!

# Excellent Explorers

You are a famous explorer in search of a rare, pink tiger.
Plan your story and write it here. What else do you encounter on your journey?

_____
_____
_____
_____
_____
_____
_____
_____
_____
_____
_____
_____
_____
_____
_____
_____
_____

You
did it!

# My Stories

Create covers for your two favorite stories in this book.

Fantastic!

On these pages, write some of your own stories.
Don't forget to use the prompts from the story arc!

# Title: _____

### THE BEGINNING
Introduce your characters and describe the setting.

### THE BUILD-UP
Introduce a potential problem and start to build the tension.

### THE PROBLEM
The problem from the previous step is now fully developed.

### THE RESOLUTION
This is where your problem needs to be resolved.

### THE ENDING
Tie up all of the loose ends to finish your story.

**Title:** _____

### THE BEGINNING
Introduce your characters and describe the setting.

### THE BUILD-UP
Introduce a potential problem and start to build the tension.

### THE PROBLEM
The problem from the previous step is now fully developed.

### THE RESOLUTION
This is where your problem needs to be resolved.

### THE ENDING
Tie up all of the loose ends to finish your story.

**Title:** _____

### THE BEGINNING
Introduce your characters and describe the setting.

### THE BUILD-UP
Introduce a potential problem and start to build the tension.

### THE PROBLEM
The problem from the previous step is now fully developed.

### THE RESOLUTION
This is where your problem needs to be resolved.

### THE ENDING
Tie up all of the loose ends to finish your story.

# Title: _____

## THE BEGINNING
Introduce your characters and describe the setting.

## THE BUILD-UP
Introduce a potential problem and start to build the tension.

## THE PROBLEM
The problem from the previous step is now fully developed.

## THE RESOLUTION
This is where your problem needs to be resolved.

## THE ENDING
Tie up all of the loose ends to finish your story.

# Title: _____

## THE BEGINNING
Introduce your characters and describe the setting.

## THE BUILD-UP
Introduce a potential problem and start to build the tension.

## THE PROBLEM
The problem from the previous step is now fully developed.

## THE RESOLUTION
This is where your problem needs to be resolved.

## THE ENDING
Tie up all of the loose ends to finish your story.

**Title:** _____

### THE BEGINNING
Introduce your characters and describe the setting.

### THE BUILD-UP
Introduce a potential problem and start to build the tension.

### THE PROBLEM
The problem from the previous step is now fully developed.

### THE RESOLUTION
This is where your problem needs to be resolved.

### THE ENDING
Tie up all of the loose ends to finish your story.

Use this page to write down any story ideas that come into your head!